kids cooking complete meals

Aileen Paul's Other Books

KIDS COOKING
(with Arthur Hawkins)
KIDS GARDENING
KIDS CAMPING
CANDIES, COOKIES, CAKES
(with Arthur Hawkins)

KIDS
COOKING
COMPLETE
MEALS

Menus, Recipes, Instructions

---

by Aileen Paul

illustrated by John Delulio

Doubleday & Company, Inc.   Garden City, New York

Library of Congress Cataloging in Publication Data

Paul, Aileen.
   Kids cooking complete meals.

   SUMMARY: A cookbook for beginning cooks which, in addition
to recipes for party, international, and family menus, supplies
information on nutrition, table setting and decorating, and other
miscellaneous aspects of cookery.
   1.   Cookery—Juvenile literature.   [1.   Cookery.
2.   Menus]   I.   Delulio, John, illus.   II.   Title.
TX652.5.P39   641.5   73-10815
ISBN 0-385-08411-0 Trade
       0-385-01938-6 Prebound
Library of Congress Catalog Card Number: 73-10815

To my aunt,
Mrs. Orpha G. Batie
of Lisco, Nebraska,
a very dear person.

contents

a word to kids

I hope you have as much fun using this book as I had working on the menus and writing the suggestions.

I have given you a wide choice of menus, some easy and some not so easy. They are planned for parties, for friends, and for family. Your choice will depend upon how much cooking you have done and your age.

Read the one you choose carefully before you begin. Talk about it and the preparation with your mother, father, or another adult. You will need some adult assistance in most cases, especially when the oven is used.

In our home we have found that each child likes to choose his or her own time for preparing a meal. I am sure that's true for you because everyone has many outside activities.

Allow plenty of time for preparation (and for cleaning up), whether it's Saturday lunch, Sunday breakfast, a week-night supper, or a party.

Whatever you choose, you need to know the cooking rules to be followed. Here are some important ones:

rules of the game

1. Turn handles of pots and pans you are using so that neither you nor anyone else will knock them off the stove or counter.

2. Use a dry pot holder when you place things in the oven and when you take them out. A damp pot holder is no protection against heat.

3. Use a paring knife (that's the little one that sometimes has a saw-toothed edge) for most of your cutting; for sandwiches use a bread knife.

4. Use a wooden chopping board for cutting. Most counter tops scratch easily.

There's one rule that the kids in my cooking classes have never broken, and I'm sure you won't either: Use the electric mixer or blender *only* when an adult is right there by you.

Adults can be useful to you in the kitchen so, depending on your age, let your "assistant" do the following:

1. Turn on the oven or the burners of the stove.

2. Stand by in case you need help when you are using the oven.

3. Pour hot water for you when needed.

There are certain steps which must be taken:

Step 1. Check the list of ingredients to be sure you have everything you need *before* you start.

Step 2. Place together the ingredients and the equipment you will need such as:

> measuring cups
> measuring spoons
> wooden spoons and rubber spatulas
> mixing bowls

Step 3. Place a damp sponge in a convenient spot to wipe up the spills that are bound to come. (Don't worry about them.)

a word to adults

As I wrote earlier in *Kids Cooking: A First Cookbook for Children,* cooking is an exciting and novel experience for children, an instant entry into the adult world.

Once a child has learned to cook a few specialties it's time to move forward to planning, preparing, and sharing a simple meal. That step allows youngsters to make choices and to understand how those food choices influence health and well-being.

There are practical results, too. A child who prepares for his or her own party, or who cooks an evening or weekend meal, makes a real contribution to family management by sharing some of the responsibility. It's a proud parent who says, "While I made some bookshelves on Saturday, my child fixed lunch."

But grownups should, of course, stay discreetly near

while the preparation goes on: to answer questions, to help with the oven, pour hot water, to give whatever assistance is needed by the young cook.

You should read the rules together and give appropriate guidance when the menu is chosen. Some menus are for beginning cooks and others for experienced junior chefs. It's helpful, I think, to make a few suggestions on utensils and equipment. What the child cooks obviously depends upon your food budget, where you live, and your style of living as well as the important fact of the child's age and learning ability.

Speaking of learning, it would be difficult, and not really desirable, to present detailed nutritional information in this book. My hope is that the "Nutritional Notes" will encourage youngsters to eat well and enjoy it.

about nutrition

Nutrition is about eating, which is fun. It's about body energy, which is important. You can have the right kind and the right amount of food each day by choosing from the following "Daily Food Guide," whether for family meals, snacks, or party foods. You will find more information in the "Food Chart" at the end of the book.

meat, poultry, fish, eggs

. . . needed—two servings a day.

. . . supply protein, which helps growth, energy, body repair.

. . . for vegetarians, additional sources of protein are peanut butter, dried beans and peas, and soybeans.

milk and dairy products

. . . needed—three or four glasses of milk or substitute.

. . . give you riboflavin, calcium, and protein.

. . . included in this group are cheese and ice cream.

vegetables and fruits

. . . needed—four or more servings a day.

. . . every day, eat a Vitamin C food oranges, grapefruit, tomatoes, cantaloupe, and others.

... every other day, eat a Vitamin A food (carrots, sweet potatoes, broccoli, and others).

... vegetables and fruits give you additional vitamins and minerals (see "Food Chart" at end of book) important directly to your body and to help make use of other foods. Apples, bananas, green beans, potatoes (to mention a few), and others should be included each day.

breads and cereals

... needed—four or more servings a day.

... a source of energy, thiamin, riboflavin, niacin, and some iron.

... included in this group are enriched, whole-grain bread and cereals, and other grain products such as corn meal, grits, macaroni, spaghetti, rice.

... a serving is 1 slice of bread, 1 cup of most ready-to-eat cereals, or ½ cup of cooked cereal.

about buying

See section "About the Number of Servings" to figure how much food you need to buy and prepare.

meat

Buy from a clean meat market of good reputation. Meat must be inspected by either the federal government or the state.

poultry

Chicken is available chilled or frozen, whole or cut up.

fish

The fish you buy may be fresh, frozen, or canned. Fresh fish can be bought whole (ask for it to be

19

cleaned) and in steaks or fillets. Most fish dealers will prepare it for cooking. Also, they can tell you what fish are in season and, therefore, which to buy.

eggs

Buy in cartons at a store where eggs are kept in re-frigerated cases. Buy Grade A or Grade AA with either brown or white shells. The color of the shells does not affect the quality. Eggs are labeled Extra Large, Large, Medium, and Small.

fresh fruits and vegetables

Try to buy those that are in season because the price is sometimes lower—apples in the fall, oranges in the winter and early spring. Here are a few ways to help you look for freshness and ripeness.

apples—good color and firmness
bananas—fresh yellow color, not too spotted
celery—clean, crisp-looking
lettuce—heads that are green, crisp, and firm

21

canned and frozen foods

Read the label carefully.

Most canned foods are packed and priced according to their quality.

Buy the highest quality in most cases. You can buy second quality (identified as "economy," "Grade B," etc.) when you are using fruits or vegetables in sauces, soups, puddings or other desserts where size, shape, or color is not important.

Buy frozen fruits and vegetables that are frozen solid. Do not buy thawed packages or packages that feel soft and are stained. Thawing and refreezing are not wise because the quality of the food is lowered.

about milk

Buy pasteurized, homogenized Vitamin D milk, or skim milk if you are concerned about your weight. Milk made from non-fat dry milk powder has a pleasant flavor when chilled. Buttermilk, made usually from pasteurized skim milk, offers a change in taste.

about storing

meat, poultry, and fish

All should be promptly refrigerated. The transparent wrap on meat, poultry, and fish should not be left on more than one or two days, preferably one. If you are keeping food longer, unwrap, place on platter or tray, and loosely cover with fresh wrap before refrigerating.

Wrap and store fish separately. Ham, frankfurters, bacon, and sausage can be stored in their containers, or loosely wrapped, in the refrigerator.

eggs

Store promptly in refrigerator, large end up.

fresh fruits and vegetables

Fresh fruits should be ripe when stored in the refrigerator. Wash just before eating. Keep bananas at room temperature. Sort berries and cherries before refrigerating, unwashed.

canned, frozen, and dried foods

Store canned food in dry place at room temperature, frozen in freezing unit or freezer, dried in tightly closed containers at room temperature.

milk

Store immediately in refrigerator. Keep container closed.

about the number of servings

Learn to buy the right amount of food so that you do not waste. It helps to know that the average serving of cooked meat per person is about 3 ounces and the average serving of fruits or vegetables is 4 ounces, or ½ cup.

servings and pounds

ITEM	SERVINGS
Meat, Poultry, and Fish, cooked	per pound
Meat with little or no bone	3 or 4
Hamburger or ground meat	4 or 5

ITEM	SERVINGS
Chicken	2 or 3
Fish Fillets	3 or 4

Vegetables, raw

Cabbage	9 or 10
Carrots	5 or 6
Celery	5 or 6
Tomatoes	4

Frozen Vegetables

per 9- or 10-ounce package

Most varieties	3 or 4

Canned Vegetables

per 1-pound can

Most varieties	3 or 4
Pork and beans with tomato sauce	2 or 3

Frozen Fruit

per 10- or 12-ounce package

Most varieties	3

Canned Fruit

per 1-pound can

Most varieties	4

Dried Fruit

per 8-ounce package

Apricots and mixed fruits	6
Peaches	7
Prunes	4 or 5

about table setting
and decorating

For a party, buffet service (serve yourself) is usually the easiest.

Arrange the table in this order: napkins, plates, hot dishes, cold dishes, bread, knives and forks. Beverages and glasses should be on a side table along with the dessert and spoons, if necessary.

party menus

before folk dancing

Encourage your community center or another organization to sponsor folk dancing for children and young people. Invite friends to supper before the dance.

MENU

Tuna on a Roll
Baked Beans
Tossed Green Salad (see Index)
Apricots and Butter Cookies
Milk

HERE'S WHAT YOU DO

1. Forty-five minutes before serving, begin preparation by turning oven temperature to 300 degrees.

Open can of baked beans in tomato sauce and pour into casserole. Add topping of grated American cheese or flavored crumbs. Place casserole in oven and heat for 30 minutes without cover.

2. Set table for self-serving.

3. While beans are baking, prepare tuna by mixing one 3-ounce package softened cream cheese and ¼ cup prepared yellow mustard in medium-sized bowl. Add 1 can (7 ounces) drained tuna and ½ cup chopped celery. Mix thoroughly. Put in center of platter with sliced rolls. Guests make their own sandwiches.

4. Prepare Tossed Green Salad and take to table.

5. Spoon canned apricots into individual serving dishes. Place on tray and carry along with small plate of cookies and pitcher of milk to table.

6. Remove casserole of baked beans from oven. Remember to use pot holders and to ask an adult for help, if needed. Place on tile or trivet on serving table.

One can (1 pound, 12 ounces) baked beans makes 4 to 6 servings.

Tuna mixture makes 4 to 6 servings

NUTRITIONAL NOTE

Foods from the bread and cereal group supply protein, carbohydrate, thiamin, riboflavin, and niacin.

For better nutrition, use bread and rolls made with enriched flour.

See "Food Chart" at end of book.

before fund raising for
your favorite organization

Money-raising projects are easier when you plan and begin them together. This meal can be a good starter, and it's easy to prepare. Divide up the work among friends. Eat in the kitchen for quick cleanup.

MENU

Cheese Frankfurters on Buns
Herbed Green Beans
Relish and Mustard
Molasses Cookies
Buttermilk

HERE'S WHAT YOU DO

1. About 30 minutes before eating, set the table, including relish, mustard, and a plate of cookies.

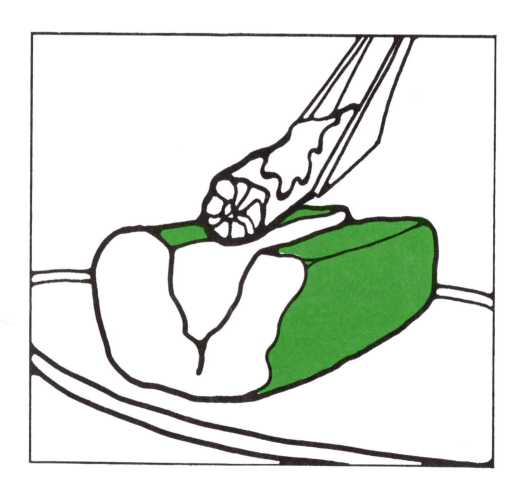

2. Using paring knife, make small slit, about 2 inches long, in each frankfurter. Fry on low to medium heat in skillet for several minutes on split side. Turn frankfurters. Carefully spoon slivers of processed cheese into slits. Increase heat to medium. Cook for 3 or 4 minutes, or until cheese is melted. Keep on simmer or warm.

3. Open can of green beans (the long, vertical ones called "Blue Lake" are excellent). Drain liquid into saucepan and add ½ teaspoon favorite dried herbs (orégano, basil, thyme). Heat over medium heat, and add green beans.

4. Use tongs or wide spatula to remove frankfurters to buns. Place on platter, pour beans into bowl, and take both to table.

5. Serve buttermilk, and dinner is ready.

NUTRITIONAL NOTE

Milk and other dairy products are needed daily to give calcium and protein.

Needed: 3 to 4 glasses daily.

Buttermilk's flavor is similar to yogurt. It has the same food value as milk but less calories than whole milk, about 90 total.

See "Food Chart" at end of book.

before a nature walk

A nice way to start the day with friends.

MENU

Grapefruit Halves with Honey
Waffles with Maple-blended Syrup
Sausages
Milk

HERE'S WHAT YOU DO THE NIGHT BEFORE

1. Set table for a sit-down breakfast.

2. Prepare grapefruit halves, add 1 tablespoon honey, cover with transparent wrap, and refrigerate.

3. Prepare waffle batter according to instructions on package of buttermilk baking mix or your own recipe. Put in pitcher or 4-cup measuring cup for easy pouring. Cover and refrigerate.

4. Place waffle iron at your place at table or on serving cart. Check working condition. Find extra extension cord if needed.

HERE'S WHAT YOU DO THE NEXT MORNING

1. Remove all items except milk from refrigerator and take butter to table.

2. Set oven temperature at 400 degrees and 10 minutes later place sausages in baking pan in oven.

36

Cook for 20 minutes, or according to time on package.

3. Wipe grids of waffle iron lightly with greased paper towel before baking. Set temperature on waffle iron.

4. Take pitcher of milk to table. Let a friend pour for you.

5. Remove pan of sausages from oven. Use pot hold-

ers. Transfer to platter with tongs and bring to table.

6. While friends eat grapefruit, start baking waffles.

NUTRITIONAL NOTE

Sugar, syrup, jams, jellies, and honey are sources of energy. They are in the carbohydrate group.

See "Food Chart" at end of book.

before youth group meeting

Many families eat their Sunday night meal a little earlier than usual. If your youth group meets on that night, start the evening with a simple dessert.

MENU

Make-Your-Own Sundaes
Fruit Punch

HERE'S WHAT YOU DO

1. Prepare a quick fruit punch by mixing equal amounts of orange juice, cranberry juice, and carbonated water. Add ice. Serve in pitcher for easier pouring.

2. Place sundae dishes, paper cups, spoons, and napkins on serving table.

3. Put containers of different ice creams on a large tray before placing on serving table. Wrap containers in foil the way florists do plants. Place several ice cream scoops nearby.

4. On another tray, place fruit toppings along with wheat germ, shelled sunflower seeds, or chopped nuts in small bowls for a nutritious garnish. People help themselves.

1 quart of ice cream makes 4 to 6 servings. Three quarts of punch make 12 large (8-ounce) glasses.

NUTRITIONAL NOTE

From the milk and dairy group we receive calcium and protein, among other things.

Regular ice cream gives you calcium and protein.

You know what calcium does—helps proper bone growth.

Keep in mind that you need about twice as much ice cream as milk for the same food value.

See "Food Chart" at end of book.

after the ball game

Everyone is hungry. Everyone needs health-giving food, and it's nice to have it look attractive.

DINNER MENU

Tomato Juice with Wheat Crackers
Baked Corned Beef Hash
Buttered Corn
Tossed Green Salad (see Index)

Rye Bread
Butter
Brownies
Milk

HERE'S WHAT YOU DO BEFORE THE GAME

1. Set serving table so that guests can help themselves.

2. Place small glasses on tray with bowl of crackers. Place tomato juice in refrigerator to chill.

3. Lightly grease two casseroles. Open cans of corned beef hash and put in one casserole.

4. Open cans of Niblets corn; drain half the liquid; empty corn into other casserole. Chop 1 green pepper and stir into corn along with several pats of butter. Cover casseroles and store in refrigerator.

5. Prepare Tossed Green Salad without dressing. Cover and refrigerate. Place salad dressing on serving table.

6. Remove brownies from freezer to defrost.

WHILE YOU ARE AT THE GAME

1. Ask an adult to turn oven heat to 325 degrees 45 minutes before serving time, which you have shown on your schedule.

2. Place corned beef hash casserole in oven 30 minutes before eating.

3. Add casserole of corn 10 minutes later.

WHEN YOU RETURN

1. Pour tomato juice and carry tray into living room. Let guests serve themselves as they arrive.

2. Cut brownies and place on platter. Take along with salad, bread, and butter, to serving table.

3. Use pot holders to remove hot casseroles. You may need an older person to help you. Place on trivets or tiles on table.

4. Pour milk. Remove wrap from salad. Toss with dressing. People serve themselves.

1 can of corned beef hash makes 3 to 4 servings

NUTRITIONAL NOTE

From the meat group we get protein. It means "first" in Greek, and it is of first importance to health. You need protein every day for energy, repair, and growth.

See "Food Chart" at end of book.

45

after ice skating

You need something hot and nourishing.

MENU

Chili Con Carne (see Index)
Carrot and Celery Sticks
Tossed Green Salad (see Index)
Crusty Bread
Butter
Oatmeal Cookies
Hot Cocoa

HERE'S WHAT YOU DO

1. Before you go, prepare Chili Con Carne. Allow 2 hours from start to finish.

2. Set table for self-serving.

3. Scrub celery and carrots. Cut into 3-inch sticks. Arrange in rows on oblong dish. Cover and refrigerate until serving time.

4. Prepare salad and refrigerate in covered bowl without dressing.

5. Mound cookies on pretty platter. Place bread in basket and take both to serving table.

6. Put ingredients for hot cocoa together in kitchen. Include an unbreakable container for serving.

BEFORE GUESTS ARRIVE

1. Heat chili in pot, preferably one that can be taken to table and placed on trivet or tray.

2. Remove refrigerator items and place on table. Toss salad.

3. Prepare hot cocoa and keep on low heat until guests arrive.

NUTRITIONAL NOTE

Salads are important for vitamins and minerals. Add other raw vegetables such as carrots, green peppers, celery, and tomatoes to lettuce.

There's a lot of protein in this meal, from the chili to the hot cocoa. You need it every day for strong bones and teeth.

See "Food Chart" at end of book.

after the school play

Your friends may be the actors, the costume makers, or that important group, the audience. However varied their participation, boys and girls are alike in enjoying food and needing it for energy.

MENU

Fancy Peanut-Cream Cheese Sandwiches
Raisin Bar Cookies (see Index)
Fruit
Molasses Milk

HERE'S WHAT YOU DO

1. Before you go, set table for self-serving with basket of washed fruit as centerpiece.

2. Bake or buy cookies. Store in covered cookie jar and place on table.

3. Make sandwiches. Use whole wheat bread with a filling of equal amounts of peanut butter and cream cheese. Remove crusts. Cut into shapes with cookie cutters. Arrange on platter, wrap in transparent plastic wrap, and place in refrigerator until serving time.

4. Pour milk into pitcher and stir in 1 cup molasses (preferably Blackstrap) per quart. Cover and refrigerate.

5. When you return home with friends, take milk and sandwiches to table. Remove wrap. Let people help themselves.

NUTRITIONAL NOTE

Raisins have a number of vitamins and minerals. The iron in raisins helps the blood cells use oxygen.

Raisins are naturally sweet, which makes them a better choice than candies.

Molasses Milk gives you an additional amount of iron.

See "Food Chart" at end of book.

after swimming

Invite friends over for a supper that's easily prepared in advance.

MENU

New Orleans Fruit Punch (see Index)
Supper Sandwich Board
Ice Cream
Banana Cake

HERE'S WHAT YOU DO

1. Before you go, set serving table so that guests can help themselves.

2. Prepare ingredients for punch, leaving ginger ale to be added at the last. Refrigerate all liquids.

3. Arrange Supper Sandwich Board by buttering slices of bread. Place on tray and layer with slices of cheese, ham, and drained pineapple rings. Top with bread. Wrap airtight. Make a dressing by mixing 1 cup mayonnaise with 1 tablespoon mustard, 1 teaspoon onion salt, and enough pineapple juice to make it thin. Place in small bowl and cover. Put both in refrigerator until serving time.

4. Remove frozen banana cake from foil to defrost. Place on pretty plate and take to serving table.

5. Spoon ice cream into paper cups for easy serving, cover with airtight Saran wrap, and keep in freezer until ready.

53

WHEN YOU RETURN

1. Remove ice and place in punch bowl. Add ingredients, including ginger ale. Stir.

2. Place Supper Sandwich Board on table with dressing, which may be spooned on by guests.

3. When it's time for dessert, bring out the ice cream.

NUTRITIONAL NOTE

The fruits in the New Orleans Punch help to meet your daily needs for Vitamins A and C.

Lemon, orange, and lime give you Vitamin C, which helps your body deal with infection and keeps your mouth healthy.

Apricot and pineapple supply Vitamin A, good for the skin, among other things.

See "Food Chart" at end of book.

international
and regional menus

from denmark

The Open-faced Sandwiches that are served in Denmark and other Scandinavian countries are fun to look at and to eat.

MENU

Open-faced Sandwiches
Fruit
Cookies
Milk

HERE'S WHAT YOU DO

1. About 20 minutes before eating, set the table. Include pitcher for milk, and knives and forks for the Open-faced Sandwiches.

2. Wash and dry fruit. Place in basket if you have one. Arrange cookies on plate. Take both to table.

3. To make Open-faced Sandwiches (best made immediately before eating), spread softened or whipped butter to edges of each slice of bread.

4. Place bread on serving platter. To each slice, add lettuce, thin slices of meat or cheese, and top with finely cut, drained beets, cucumbers, tomatoes, or other vegetable. The vegetable colors should contrast with the meat and cheese.

5. Pour milk.

NUTRITIONAL NOTE

Serve fruit uncooked and unpeeled whenever possible. Wash quickly (never soak fruit) as close to mealtime as you can.

If fruits are chopped, that, too, should be done close to the time of eating.

By following these suggestions, you will keep vitamins at their best.

See "Food Chart" at end of book.

from hawaii

Hawaii, one of our new states, offers native food and food influenced by the many races who live there—Japanese, Chinese, and Filipino.

The "luau" is the Hawaiian celebration feast. Flowers, food, music, and dancing are part of it. Most of us cannot gather tropical fruit or "roast a pig" (a feature of the luau), but we can still give a Hawaiian party.

MENU

Hawaiian Hamburgers (see Index)
Pineapple Cabbage Salad
Rice
Fruit with "Wiki Wiki"
Hawaiian Punch Bowl

HERE'S WHAT YOU DO

1. Early in the day, prepare Hawaiian Hamburgers according to recipe. Cover and refrigerate uncooked.

2. Make American version of coconut pudding ("Wiki Wiki") by using instant coconut cream pudding mix. Cover and place in refrigerator.

3. Set a large serving table in the Hawaiian style. Mound fresh fruit in the center. Tuck in sea shells, if you have any, large green leaves or small green potted plants, flowers if available.

ABOUT 30 MINUTES BEFORE EATING

1. Make Pineapple Cabbage Salad. Use food chopper or grater with large holes to shred 2 cups cabbage. Drain 2 cups crushed pineapple. Add to cabbage. Sprinkle with prepared French dressing and mix thoroughly. Arrange lettuce leaves in wooden bowl and spoon Pineapple Cabbage Salad into center. Top with chopped salted peanuts. Place on table.

2. Drain hamburgers and cook according to recipe. Keep on low heat until served.

3. Cook Minute Rice, following instructions on package. Also keep on low heat until served.

4. Before serving, put ice in the punch bowl. Pour over ice 1 can (1 quart 14 ounces) prepared Hawaiian Punch and ½ quart bottle club soda. Double amount if needed. Float thin slices lemon or orange on top as decoration.

5. When ready to eat, mound rice in center of large platter, surround with hamburgers, pour on sauce. Take to table along with bowl of "Wiki Wiki."

Pineapple Cabbage Salad makes 4 servings

NUTRITIONAL NOTE

From the vegetable-fruit group, this menu gives you raw cabbage, which is high in Vitamin C, and carrots, which have Vitamin A. You need at least 1 serving each day for the right amount of Vitamin C, and 1 serving every other day for Vitamin A.

See "Food Chart" at end of book.

from mexico

Mexican food is fun because it's different and color-ful. Mexican families were handing down favorite rec-ipes from family to family early in their history. Mock Tamale Pie is something like the food that was served thousands of years ago at holiday time.

National and local holidays are celebrated with fiestas. Plan your Mexican party around their Independence Day, which runs from the night of September 15 through September 16.

MENU

Mock Tamale Pie (see Index)
Salad
Chocolate Pudding
Fruit Juice

HERE'S WHAT YOU DO

1. About 1 hour before serving, cook Mock Tamale Pie.

2. Set table for self-serving.

3. Make chocolate pudding with instant pudding mix. Pour into individual serving dishes and place on table.

4. Prepare an easy version of the Mexican Christmas Eve salad by adding a small amount of drained diced or sliced canned beets and 1 chopped orange to a Tossed Green Salad (see Index). Add salad dressing and place on table.

5. Pour juice into pitcher and take to table.

6. If you cooked the tamale pie in an attractive pot, take directly to table for serving. Clean around edge with paper towel. Remember to use pot holders and place on trivet on serving table.

NUTRITIONAL NOTE

Corn meal in the Mock Tamale Pie belongs, of course, to the grouping of breads and cereals, since it is a grain.

Needed: Several servings a day from that group.

Corn meal is a source of Vitamin A.

See "Food Chart" at end of book.

from switzerland

*Being a good cook is important in Switzerland. Fami-
lies have their own favorite recipes which may be
slightly different from canton to canton (a canton is
a Swiss state).*

*The main meal is eaten in the middle of the day, a
light supper at night, and a snack about 4 P.M. at which
hot tea is served if the weather is cold. You might invite several of your favorite grownups for a Swiss tea.*

MENU

Crusty Bread
Swiss Cheese
Swiss Filled Cupcakes
Hot Tea (see Index) or Apple Juice

HERE'S WHAT YOU DO

1. Start about an hour before teatime and prepare Swiss Filled Cupcakes by baking chocolate cupcakes from a prepared mix.

2. While they are baking, set table, using your prettiest cloth and dishes, some flowers if you have them.

3. After cupcakes are cooled, cut out small cone of cake at the top, using serrated-edge paring knife. Mix 1½ cups raspberry jam and 1½ cups finely chopped almonds. Spoon into hole in cake. Replace a small part of the top and sprinkle with confectioners' sugar. Arrange on attractive serving dish.

4. Place water on to boil and follow instructions on tea making. You may need adult help.

5. While water is heating, slice bread on chopping board and place on platter along with Swiss cheese. (Crusty bread means French or Italian bread. There is a delicious and crusty Swiss bread but it is available only in specialty bakeries.)

6. As soon as your guests arrive, complete tea making and serve, pouring carefully.

NUTRITIONAL NOTE

Cheese belongs to the milk and dairy products group.

Cheese provides calcium. And calcium, in addition to building bones and teeth, helps nerves, muscles, and heart to work properly.

1 serving of cheese (1¼ ounces) equals 1 cup of milk in calcium.

See "Food Chart" at end of book.

from new england

Almost everything on the menu comes from the countryside of New England. But probably you will have to do your harvesting in the local supermarket.

MENU

Cranberry Juice
Red Flannel Hash
Rolls
Butter
Apples
Milk

HERE'S WHAT YOU DO

1. About 30 minutes before eating, make Red Flannel Hash. Combine 1 cup chopped canned corned beef, 1 cup canned diced beets, and 3 cups chopped leftover boiled potatoes (or canned). Melt 1 tablespoon butter or margarine in fry pan; stir in meat and vegetables. Sprinkle with 1 teaspoon onion salt and add ½ cup beef consomme. Mash together. Brown over medium heat about 20 minutes.

2. Set table, including rolls, butter, and ketchup or chili sauce for Red Flannel Hash.

3. Pour cranberry juice in glasses in kitchen and take to table along with pitcher of milk.

4. Wash and polish apples. Arrange in basket. Use as centerpiece on table.

5. When hash is brown on bottom (lift edge with spatula after about 15 minutes to check and turn up heat if necessary), place upside down on plate or platter.

Red Flannel Hash makes 4 to 6 servings

NUTRITIONAL NOTE

From the fruit and vegetable group, beets and apples have a variety of vitamins and minerals.

A small amount of fats, such as butter, margarine, oil, are needed in your daily diet for energy, and to help the body use other nutrients.

See "Food Chart" at end of book.

from the south

Ham and grits and hot breads are favorites in the South. They are good foods for a party brunch, or as a morning meal.

MENU

Orange Juice
Buttered Grits
Ham Slice (see Index)
Hot Coffee Cake
Milk

HERE'S WHAT YOU DO

1. Begin preparation about an hour before. Grits are easily prepared. Bring 4 cups water to boil in saucepan, add 1 teaspoon salt, slowly pour in 1 cup grits. Stir until mixture comes to boil, then lower heat immediately. Cover and simmer about 1 hour, stirring frequently.

2. Bake quick coffee cake by following instructions on package of biscuit mix. Add ½ cup wheat germ to ingredients. To topping, add ⅓ cup wheat germ for additional nutrition.

3. Pan-fry ham according to recipe—see Index.

4. While food is cooking, rinse dishes and pans used. Place in sink and cover with warm soapy water. Washing will be easier later.

5. Set table, including butter. Pour orange juice and milk.

6. Remove coffee cake from oven. Remember to use pot holders. You may need adult help. Empty on plate and cover immediately with small clean towel or cloth napkin to keep warm.

7. Empty grits into bowl; place ham on platter.

8. Take all three to table.

NUTRITIONAL NOTE

Wheat germ is the most nutritious part of the wheat. It is rich in protein, B vitamins, iron, and vitamin E.

You can add it to other foods, as we did in the coffee cake or eat it as a cereal.

See "Food Chart" at end of book.

from the west

As I said in the beginning, some of the menus are for
younger cooks, some for older. Because of the double
use of the oven, I recommend the following for older
junior chefs.

MENU

Baked Spareribs with Sauce
Taco Beans
Sliced Raw Vegetables
Rye Bread
Butter
Lemon Pudding
Milk

HERE'S WHAT YOU DO

1. About 90 minutes before eating, bake spareribs. Place oven racks far enough apart to hold spareribs and baked beans. Turn oven to 500 degrees. Place spareribs on small rack in uncovered roasting pan. Put in oven (use pot holders); turn heat down to 325 degrees.

2. Bake 1 hour. During last 30 minutes, cover ribs with prepared barbecue sauce twice.

3. Prepare Taco Beans by combining 1 can (1 pound, 12 ounces) baked beans, 1 large can drained, crushed pineapple, 1 can (8 ounces) tomato sauce, 1 cup coarsely crushed tortilla chips, ½ cup grated Cheddar cheese, 1 teaspoon onion salt, and 1 teaspoon chili powder. Pour into shallow baking pan and put in oven on second rack 40 minutes before spareribs are finished.

4. Set table, including butter.

5. Prepare lemon pudding, following directions on package of instant pudding, and spoon into individual serving dishes. Place on table.

6. Slice whatever vegetables are in season: tomatoes, green peppers, cucumbers. Arrange on platter. Take to table along with bread and milk.

7. Carefully remove roasting pan from oven when ribs have finished cooking, and place on wooden

board, or asbestos pad, or other heatproof area. Use two cooking forks to remove ribs to platter.

8. Take Taco Beans from oven directly to table and place on trivet or tile.

Taco Beans makes 4 servings

NUTRITIONAL NOTE

You have noticed that we serve milk with almost every meal. While you are growing, you need more of the important protective things in food such as calcium, riboflavin, and protein. Milk and other dairy products are the simplest, most practical way to get them.

See "Food Chart" at end of book.

family menus

eggs for breakfast

The easiest way to cook them is to boil them.

MENU

Tomato Juice
Eggs
Buttered Toast and Jam
Milk

HERE'S WHAT YOU DO

1. Put eggs in saucepan; cover them completely with cold water. Place pan on medium heat and bring water to boil.

2. For soft-cooked eggs, cover pan and remove from heat once the boiling has begun. Let stand 5 minutes.

3. For hard-cooked eggs, after water has come to a boil, lower heat and simmer (that is, keep just below boiling) for 10 to 15 minutes.

4. While eggs are cooking, set the table. Pour tomato juice and milk.

5. As soon as eggs are cooked, remove from water

(a slotted spoon is helpful). Place in individual bowls or egg cups. Take to table.

6. Toast bread, butter it, and call everyone to breakfast.

NUTRITIONAL NOTE

From the meat, poultry, fish, egg group, you need 2 servings a day. The protein in eggs is complete, that is, has the necessary protein for building and rebuilding your body.

Eggs also contain important vitamins and minerals.

See "Food Chart" at end of book.

french toast for breakfast

I think everyone likes French Toast. Have you ever known anyone who did not?

MENU

Mandarin Oranges
French Toast
Syrup
Milk

HERE'S WHAT YOU DO

1. Set the table, including pitcher of syrup.

2. Open can of mandarin oranges and spoon into individual small dishes. Place on table.

3. To make French Toast: break 2 eggs into bowl and add ⅓ cup milk, 1 tablespoon sugar, ⅛ teaspoon salt, ½ teaspoon vanilla. Beat until blended.

4. Place frying pan on medium heat and add butter or margarine to cover bottom of pan when melted.

5. Dip pieces of bread into egg mixture. Place in skillet. Fry until golden brown on one side, turn and fry on the other. Add more butter to pan if needed.

6. Serve and let your family eat immediately.

2-egg French Toast makes 4 or 5 servings

NUTRITIONAL NOTE

Most of us are used to drinking orange juice for the daily Vitamin C we need. And that's great. But if you want a change, serve mandarin oranges (chilled, if there's time) or canned grapefruit and orange sections.

Vitamin C helps in healing wounds, in bone growth, in holding the body cells together.

See "Food Chart" at end of book.

muffins for breakfast

Muffins are easy to make. They can be baked that morning, the night before, or at any time in advance and frozen.

MENU

Orange Juice
Cereal
Muffins
Grape Jelly
Milk

HERE'S WHAT YOU DO

1. About 45 minutes before eating, turn over perature to 400 degrees.

2. Beat 1 egg, 1 cup milk, and ⅓ cup vegetable oil with fork or egg beater. Into separate bowl measure 1¼ cups flour, 1 tablespoon baking powder, 1 teaspoon salt, 1 cup quick-cooking oatmeal, and ½ cup raisins. Stir gently to blend ingredients. Add egg mixture to flour and stir with mixing spoon until moistened.

3. Do not beat with electric mixer. Do not overbeat. Batter should be lumpy. Grease muffin tins and fill half full of batter. Bake 20 to 25 minutes.

4. While muffins are baking, wash bowls and utensils used.

5. Set the table. Include butter, grape jelly, cereal, sugar, and pitcher of milk.

6. Pour orange juice and milk.

7. Remove muffins from oven when done, using pot holders. Place in basket or bowl and cover with clean small towel or napkin to keep hot.

Muffin recipe makes 12

NUTRITIONAL NOTE

There are many ways of getting the four daily servings needed from the bread-cereal group.

Muffins are one way. If made with enriched flour (check package) and oatmeal, they provide protein, vitamins, minerals, and energy. Adding raisins, blueberries, or nuts makes the muffins taste even better and also adds to the food value.

See "Food Chart" at end of book.

salad lunch

Easy to plan ahead and nice for summer days.

MENU

Potato Salad
Sliced Bologna or Salami
Tossed Green Salad (see Index)
Brown Bread and Cream Cheese Sandwiches
Cookies
Milk

HERE'S WHAT YOU DO

1. Set table, and begin cooking about 30 minutes before eating.

2. Prepare Potato Salad by mixing 6 diced medium-sized leftover boiled potatoes (remove skins), ¼ cup chopped green pepper, ¾ cup finely chopped celery, ¼ cup sweet pickle relish, and 2 or 3 chopped hard-cooked eggs.

3. Combine ½ cup mayonnaise, 1 tablespoon prepared yellow mustard, and 2½ teaspoons onion salt. Spoon over potato mixture. Stir, do not mash, with fork until blended.

4. Place Potato Salad on large platter surrounded by sliced bologna, salami, or other luncheon meats (called "cold cuts") of your choice.

5. Prepare Tossed Green Salad.

6. Slice brown bread and spread with whipped cream cheese for sandwiches.

Potato Salad makes 6 servings

NUTRITIONAL NOTE

Potatoes should always be cooked with skins on to keep the protein, vitamins, and minerals. They support growth and health.

See "Food Chart" at end of book.

soup and hot corn bread for lunch

You can make Corn Bread from a packaged mix or from the beginning.

MENU

Bean with Bacon Soup
Sliced Tomatoes on Lettuce
Corn Bread
Bananas
Milk

HERE'S WHAT YOU DO

1. About 35 minutes before eating, turn oven temperature to 400 degrees.

2. To prepare Corn Bread: Mix 1 cup yellow corn meal, 1 cup flour, 4 teaspoons baking powder, ⅓ cup sugar, and ½ teaspoon salt.

3. Combine 1 cup milk, 1 egg, and ¼ cup vegetable oil. Beat. Add liquid to dry ingredients. Stir only enough to mix. Pour batter into greased 8 x 2-inch baking pan. Bake 25 minutes.

4. While Corn Bread is baking, set table. Remember soup spoons and butter.

5. Heat soup according to instructions on package or can. Simmer, do not boil.

6. Slice tomatoes on chopping board. Arrange on lettuce leaves on plate. Take to table along with basket of bananas and pitcher of milk.

7. Remove corn bread from oven. Use pot holders. Turn upside down on plate. Take to table before cutting, to keep hot.

8. Pour soup into bowls.

1 can of soup makes 3 or 4 servings
Corn Bread makes 10 to 12 servings

NUTRITIONAL NOTE

Bean soup, a source of protein, counts as one of the two servings needed daily from the meat, poultry, fish, egg group.

In addition, bean soup supplies some Vitamin A which, among other things, keeps the lining of the mouth, nose, and throat healthy.

See "Food Chart" at end of book.

soup and sandwiches for lunch

Even if the lunch is simple, set a nice-looking table for your family.

MENU

Chicken with Rice Soup
Make-Your-Own Sandwiches
Apples and Cheese
Milk

HERE'S WHAT YOU DO

1. About 15 minutes before eating, set table. Include soup bowls and spoons.

2. For Make-Your-Own Sandwiches, place stacks of sliced bread on a large platter or tray. In the center, put matching containers (Pyrex custard cups do nicely) of peanut butter, jelly, pickle relish, sliced bananas, cream cheese—unusual but great go-togethers.

3. Take to table.

4. Follow instructions carefully on can or package of soup for heating. Use low to medium heat. Remember—prepared soup is already cooked.

5. Arrange apples on plate along with wedge or block of Cheddar or Swiss cheese.

6. Pour milk and soup. Everyone makes his or her own sandwiches.

NUTRITIONAL NOTE

Peanut butter ranks high in a wide variety of things you need for good health.

It is an excellent source of protein. When you combine it with fruit, some of the important vitamins are added.

See "Food Chart" at end of book.

cheese fondue for dinner

MENU

Cheese Fondue (see Index)
Peas
Coleslaw
Applesauce
Milk

HERE'S WHAT YOU DO

1. About an hour before mealtime, prepare the easy Cheese Fondue.

2. Set table, including pitcher for milk.

3. Make Coleslaw by shredding 3 cups cabbage and mixing it with ¼ cup chopped green pepper and ½ cup chopped celery. Sprinkle with prepared French dressing and mix. Spoon into bowl and place on table.

4. Pour applesauce into pretty individual dishes and sprinkle with ground nutmeg or small amount of cinnamon.

5. Clean up dishes and utensils you have used for preparation. Always wipe counter areas and chopping boards with clean sponges or paper towels.

6. About 5 minutes before fondue is ready, prepare frozen peas according to instructions. Do not overcook. Boil in recommended amount of water.

7. Pour milk.

8. Remove fondue from oven. Use pot holders. You may need adult help. Carry to table and place on trivet or tile.

9. Empty peas into serving dish, top with small piece of butter, take to table.

Coleslaw makes 6 servings and so does the Cheese Fondue

NUTRITIONAL NOTE

From the fruit and vegetable group, this menu offers an excellent variety, as you can see.

Green peas contain Vitamin A, which helps growth, and Vitamin C, which is needed to make and keep the material that holds body cells together.

See "Food Chart" at end of book.

chicken for dinner

Chicken is generally priced lower than meat. It's smart, then, to serve it frequently. For the following recipe, buy one frying chicken cut in pieces. If the breast is not cut in half, ask the butcher to do so. The pieces are then equal in size for even baking.

MENU

Chicken Easy
Mashed Potatoes
Wax Beans
Rye Bread
Butter
Banana Pudding
Milk

HERE'S WHAT YOU DO

1. About an hour before eating, turn oven temperature to 350 degrees. Place pieces of chicken in greased baking pan, skin side down. Mix together 1 can (8 ounces) tomato sauce, ¼ cup prepared yellow mustard, and ¼ cup honey. Pour over chicken. Bake, uncovered, 30 minutes.

2. While chicken is baking, prepare banana pudding from instant pudding mix. Add sliced bananas. Cover them completely with pudding to stop discoloring. Spoon into individual dessert dishes.

3. After chicken has cooked for 30 minutes, remove pan (use pot holders) and place on heatproof area. Turn each piece of chicken. Spoon sauce from pan over it. Return to oven for 30 minutes.

4. Set table. Include bread, butter, dessert.

5. Open can of wax beans. Drain liquid into saucepan. Heat. Add beans and lower heat.

6. Prepare instant mashed potatoes according to instructions on package. Keep warm.

7. When chicken is done, remove from oven and place on table on tile or trivet.

8. Heap potatoes in bowl. Empty wax beans into dish and take both to table.

9. Pour milk.

   Chicken Easy makes 4 to 6 servings

NUTRITIONAL NOTE

Chicken has a high protein count, is low in calories, and a good source of B vitamins and Vitamin A.

See "Food Chart" at end of book

hamburgers for dinner

Hamburgers on Enriched Rolls
Broccoli
Carrot Sticks
Peaches
Milk

HERE'S WHAT YOU DO

1. About 30 minutes before eating, set the table, including mustard or ketchup, whatever your family likes, and a pitcher for milk. Preparation time is about 30 minutes.

2. Make hamburgers. Divide 1 pound ground boneless chuck into 4 equal parts and make fairly thin patties. Grease skillet lightly and fry hamburgers over medium heat until brown on one side; turn, brown on other side. Lower heat. Entire cooking time: 5 to 8 minutes for rare, 10 to 15 minutes for well done.

3. While hamburgers are sizzling, prepare frozen broccoli according to instructions on package.

4. Wash and slice carrot sticks. A paring knife (that's the shortest one) is easy to handle. Stand carrots in a thin pretty glass and put on table.

5. Open can of peaches and spoon into individual serving dishes. Top with toasted wheat germ or chopped nuts. Take to table.

6. Fill glasses and pitcher with milk.

7. When hamburgers are done, place on rolls on large platter. Add butter to cooked broccoli and pour into serving dish. Take to table.

NUTRITIONAL NOTE

Broccoli has some of the vitamins and minerals needed daily.

See "Food Chart" at end of book.

oven-fried fish for dinner

MENU

Oven-fried Fish
Buttered Beets
Potato Chips
Lettuce Wedges
Rye Bread
Butter
Grapefruit and Orange Cup
Milk

HERE'S WHAT YOU DO

1. About 30 minutes before mealtime, set the table. Include bowl of potato chips, butter and bread (you can wrap bread in transparent Saran wrap if room is dry).

2. To oven-fry fish: turn oven temperature to 500 degrees. Grease baking dish. Pour ½ cup milk into shallow bowl. Stir in 1 teaspoon salt. Put 2 cups fine bread crumbs into another shallow bowl next to first one. Dip each piece of fish (4 inches is a good length) into milk, roll in crumbs, place in

single layer (skin side down) on baking pan. Pour ¼ cup melted butter or oil over fish.

3. Place baking dish in oven. You will need adult help because the oven is very hot.

4. Bake 10 to 15 minutes. Fish is done when it flakes easily with fork.

5. While fish is in oven, prepare buttered beets. Drain liquid into saucepan and heat on medium heat. Add beets and pat of butter; continue heating.

6. Put lettuce wedges on large platter and place on table along with prepared salad dressing.

7. Spoon grapefruit and orange sections from can or jar into individual dishes and put at each place.

8. When fish is done (remember not to overcook), ask an adult to remove dish from oven and place on trivet or tile on table.

9. Pour vegetables in bowl and take to table, along with pitcher of milk.

2 pounds of fish makes about 6 servings

NUTRITIONAL NOTE

Needed: 2 servings a day from the meat, poultry, fish, egg group.

In addition to top-quality protein, fish supplies niacin, which helps the body use oxygen and helps to keep the skin and nervous system in good condition.

See "Food Chart" at end of book.

Recipes

chili con carne

3 tablespoons vegetable oil
1 pound ground boneless beef (chuck)
1 can (8 ounces) tomato sauce
1 can (1 pound) red kidney beans
    Spices
½ teaspoon celery salt
1 teaspoon onion salt
¼ teaspoon red pepper
1 tablespoon chili powder
1 bay leaf
¼ teaspoon basil
½ teaspoon caraway seed (may be omitted)

HERE'S WHAT YOU DO

1. Pour oil into large frying pan and place over medium heat. Use only enough oil to cover bottom.

2. Add ground beef and cook until beef loses red color, about 3 to 5 minutes.

3. While beef is cooking, measure spices into a cup.

4. Add tomato sauce and spices to beef.

5. Cover and cook on low heat for 1 hour or more.

6. Add red kidney beans and heat 10 minutes.

7. Taste and add additional seasonings, including salt, if needed.

Makes 4 to 6 servings

fried ham slice

HERE'S WHAT YOU NEED

1 center-cut ham slice, ¼ to ½ inch thick
(*Ham slices are often prepackaged at the meat counter*)
frying pan that's large enough, with cover
paring knife
tongs or long-handled fork

HERE'S WHAT YOU DO

1. Place frying pan over medium heat.

2. Trim fat from ham slice, leaving about ⅛ inch of fat on edge. Cut into edge of fat, every inch around,

to keep ham from curling. Place trimmed fat in frying pan. Stir with kitchen fork for 2 or 3 minutes while fat melts.

3. Remove pieces of unmelted fat from frying pan and put in ham slice.

4. Fry on one side 3 to 5 minutes for uncooked ham. Turn and fry same time on other side. (If ham is precooked, fry 2 minutes on each side.)

1 pound of ham serves 2 people generously

cheese fondue

HERE'S WHAT YOU NEED

12 slices white bread
¾ pound thinly sliced Cheddar cheese
3 eggs
3 cups milk
½ teaspoon salt
¼ teaspoon pepper
1 tablespoon butter or margarine

HERE'S WHAT YOU DO

1. Grease an 8 x 12-inch baking dish.

2. Preheat oven to 350 degrees.

3. Trim crusts from bread and lay 6 slices in dish.

4. Cover with cheese. Top with remaining bread.

5. Combine eggs and milk. Add seasonings. Beat lightly.

6. Pour over bread. Dot with butter or margarine.

7. Bake 45 minutes to 1 hour.

Makes 4 to 6 servings

hawaiian hamburgers

HERE'S WHAT YOU NEED

1 pound ground boneless beef (chuck)
3 tablespoons soy sauce
2 tablespoons vegetable oil
2 tablespoons chili sauce
1 tablespoon vinegar

HERE'S WHAT YOU DO

1. Make 4 to 6 flat patties from ground boneless beef and place in shallow baking pan.

2. To make sauce, combine soy sauce, oil, chili sauce, and vinegar.

3. Pour mixture over hamburgers, cover with airtight wrap, and refrigerate until about 20 minutes before eating.

4. At that time, remove hamburgers from refrigerator and drain. Rub frying pan lightly with shortening and heat pan over medium heat. Place meat patties in pan. Brown on one side. Turn with spatula and brown on other side.

5. Immediately lower heat, pour sauce over patties, and continue cooking about 10 minutes.

Makes 4 to 6 servings

new orleans fruit punch

HERE'S WHAT YOU NEED

2 cups sugar
⅓ cup dried mint leaves
¼ cup lemon juice, fresh or bottled
1 can (12 ounces) apricot nectar
1 can (6 ounces) frozen orange juice
1 can (6 ounces) frozen limeade
1 cup pineapple juice
2 large bottles (28 ounces) ginger ale
orange slices

HERE'S WHAT YOU DO

1. Bring 2 cups water to boil. You may need adult help.

2. Pour sugar and mint leaves in heatproof bowl (or teapot) and add boiling water. (Again you may need adult help.) Stir until sugar is dissolved.

3. Pour lemon juice, apricot nectar, frozen orange juice, limeade, and pineapple juice into punch bowl.

4. Strain mint-flavored liquid into large punch bowl. Stir.

5. If not serving punch immediately, pour blended juices into containers and store in refrigerator.

6. Before serving, remove from refrigerator, pour into punch bowl, add ginger ale and ice.

7. Add thin slices of orange to make it look pretty.

   Makes 20 to 25 small servings

mock tamale pie

HERE'S WHAT YOU NEED

2 tablespoons vegetable oil
1 chopped onion or 3 tablespoons dehydrated onions
1 pound ground boneless beef (chuck)
2 cups fresh or canned tomatoes
2 cups canned drained Niblets corn
1 cup uncooked yellow corn meal
1 cup milk
1½ tablespoons chili powder
1 teaspoon salt
1 cup grated Cheddar cheese

HERE'S WHAT YOU DO

1. Turn oven to 350 degrees.

2. Heat oil in heavy frying pan over medium heat. Add onion and beef. Cook until lightly brown.

3. Add tomatoes, corn, corn meal, milk, chili powder, and salt. Mix well.

4. Pour into greased casserole.

5. Cover and bake for 30 minutes. Uncover and sprinkle with grated Cheddar cheese. Cook uncovered for about 10 minutes.

Serves 6 to 8

raisin bar cookies

HERE'S WHAT YOU NEED

1 cup dates
1 cup nuts
1 cup (2 sticks) butter or margarine
½ cup light or dark molasses
½ cup brown sugar
4 eggs
2 cups flour
1 cup wheat germ
2 teaspoons baking powder
½ teaspoon salt (if butter is salted, reduce to ¼
        teaspoon)
1 cup rolled oats (called oatmeal)
small amount of shortening to grease pan

HERE'S WHAT YOU DO

1. Preheat oven to 350 degrees.

2. Chop dates and nuts.

3. Grease 13 x 9-inch baking pan.

4. Beat butter or margarine in electric mixer until soft and creamy. Gradually blend in molasses and sugar.

5. Add eggs, one at a time. Beat lightly.

6. Measure flour, wheat germ, baking powder, salt, and oats into 4-cup measuring cup (or small bowl) and mix gently with fork or spoon.

7. Add flour mixture, dates, and nuts to mixing bowl. Beat until blended.

8. Spread evenly in baking pan, using table knife or metal spatula. Bake for 30 minutes, or until done.

9. Cool in pan. Cut into approximately 1 x 2-inch bars.

tea

HERE'S WHAT YOU NEED

tea leaves or tea bags
teapot

HERE'S WHAT YOU DO

1. Bring fresh water to a full rolling boil in teakettle.

2. Just before making the tea, pour small amount of hot water into teapot to warm it. Pour that water out.

3. Place the amount of tea needed in the teapot. The

usual amount is 1 teaspoon tea leaves per cup, or 1 tea bag.

4. Add boiling water to tea. You will probably need adult help. Cover. Steep (which means let water remain on tea) for 3 to 5 minutes.

5. Remove tea bag and pour, or pour through strainer to remove leaves.

tossed green salad

HERE'S WHAT YOU NEED

salad greens of your choice:
    iceberg, Bibb, or Boston lettuce
celery
radishes
cucumbers
tomatoes

HERE'S WHAT YOU DO

1. Wash head of lettuce under faucet, using coldest water. Pat dry gently with paper towel. Discard outer lettuce leaves if discolored or bruised. Wrap head of lettuce in paper towel or cloth towel to absorb moisture. Chill in refrigerator if there is time.

2. Place lettuce, torn into bite-size pieces, in salad bowl.

3. Add vegetables, as many as you choose. Scrub them with vegetable brush under running cold water. Dry with paper towels. Chop on wooden board and add to greens.

4. If you are preparing in advance, cover bowl with transparent plastic wrap (make it airtight) and refrigerate until ready to use.

5. Just before serving, sprinkle with prepared salad dressing (or your own mixture) and toss.

more information

You can get more help in planning and preparing meals from booklets printed by the Office of Information, U. S. Department of Agriculture, Washington, D.C. 20250.

Write to that office on a post card and ask for a list of booklets available. You can then choose those you want. The next step is to write a letter asking for the booklet by name or number and enclose the money. They cost very little, from 15¢ up to 45¢. You can tape the coins to a piece of cardboard.

Some of the booklets may be at your library in the "Vertical File." Ask the librarian.

food chart–value of foods

A peanut butter sandwich, a glass of chocolate milk, an apple . . . what food value does each one have? The answers for most of the foods listed in the menus in this book will be found in the "Food Chart," which follows. The important facts for you are the food values so that you can compare kinds and amounts of nutrition contained in different foods.

We have taken the information from Bulletin No. 72 entitled "Nutritive Value of Foods" published by the United States Department of Agriculture. It contains about 615 foods.

If an item is not listed in our chart, it is because the food in question is a prepared food not listed in Bulletin No. 72.

The foods are under main headings: Milk; eggs; meat, poultry, and fish; dry beans and peas, nuts; vegetables; fruits; grain products; fats; sugars; and miscellaneous items.

The weight in grams is shown, and the cup measure is the standard 8-ounce measuring cup.

Calories are shown in the column headed "Food Energy."

Many items, such as ready-to-eat breakfast cereals, have nutrients added. Such information will be on the label of the package and may be different from the values shown here.

NUTRITIVE VALUES OF THE EDIBLE PARTS OF FOODS

Food, approximate measure, and weight (in grams)		Food Energy	Protein	Fat	Carbo-hydrate	Cal-cium	Iron	Vita-min A	Thia-min	Ribo-flavin	Nia-cin	Vitamin C
	Grams	Calories	Grams	Grams	Grams	Milli-grams	Milli-grams	Inter-national units	Milli-grams	Milli-grams	Milli-grams	Milli-grams
Milk, Cheese, Cream, Related Products												
Milk:												
Fluid:												
Whole, 3.5% fat . . . . 1 cup	244	160	9	9	12	288	.1	350	.07	.41	0.2	2
Non-fat (skim) . . . . 1 cup	245	90	9	Trace	12	296	.1	10	.09	.44	.2	2
Buttermilk:												
Fluid, cultured, made from skim milk . . . . . . 1 cup	245	90	9	Trace	12	296	.1	10	.10	.44	.2	2
Cheese:												
Natural:												
Cheddar:												
Ounce . . . . 1 oz.	28	115	7	9	1	213	.3	370	.01	.13	Trace	0
Cream:												
Package of, 3-oz. net wt. . . . . 1 pkg.	85	320	7	32	2	53	.2	1,310	.02	.20	.1	0
Swiss:												
Ounce . . . . 1 oz.	28	105	8	8	1	262	.3	320	Trace	.11	Trace	0
Pasteurized processed cheese:												
American:												
Ounce . . . . 1 oz.	28	105	7	9	1	198	.3	350	.01	.12	Trace	0
Swiss:												
Ounce . . . . 1 oz.	28	100	8	8	1	251	.3	310	Trace	.11	Trace	0
Cream:												
Half-and-half (cream and milk) . . . . 1 cup	242	325	8	28	11	261	.1	1,160	.07	.39	.1	2

Food	Measure	g	Calories	Protein (g)	Fat (g)	Carbohydrate (g)	Calcium (mg)	Iron (mg)	Vitamin A (IU)	Thiamine (mg)	Riboflavin (mg)	Niacin (mg)	Ascorbic acid (mg)
Milk beverage: Cocoa, homemade	1 cup	250	245	10	12	27	295	1.0	400	.10	.45	.5	3
Milk dessert: Ice cream: Regular (approx. 10% fat)	½ gal.	1,064	2,055	48	113	221	1,553	.5	4,680	.43	2.23	1.1	11

Eggs

Food	Measure	g	Calories	Protein (g)	Fat (g)	Carbohydrate (g)	Calcium (mg)	Iron (mg)	Vitamin A (IU)	Thiamine (mg)	Riboflavin (mg)	Niacin (mg)	Ascorbic acid (mg)
Eggs, large, 24 oz. per dozen: Raw or cooked in shell or with nothing added: Whole, without shell	1 egg	50	80	6	6	Trace	27	1.1	590	.05	.15	Trace	0

Meat, Poultry, Fish, Shellfish; Related Products

Food	Measure	g	Calories	Protein (g)	Fat (g)	Carbohydrate (g)	Calcium (mg)	Iron (mg)	Vitamin A (IU)	Thiamine (mg)	Riboflavin (mg)	Niacin (mg)	Ascorbic acid (mg)
Hamburger (ground beef), broiled: Lean	3 oz.	85	185	23	10	0	10	3.0	20	.08	.20	5.1	—
Regular	3 oz.	85	245	21	17	0	9	2.7	30	.07	.18	4.6	—
Corned beef hash	3 oz.	85	155	7	10	9	11	1.7	—	.01	.08	1.8	—
Chicken, cooked: Breast, fried, ½ breast: Flesh and skin only	2.7 oz.	76	155	25	5	1	9	1.3	70	.04	.17	11.2	—
Drumstick, fried: Flesh and skin only	1.3 oz.	38	90	12	4	Trace	6	.9	50	.03	.15	2.7	—
Chili con carne: With beans	1 cup	250	335	19	15	30	80	4.2	150	.08	.18	3.2	—
Ham:	3 oz.	85	245	18	19	0	8	2.2	0	.40	.16	3.1	—
Luncheon meat: Boiled ham, sliced	2 oz.	57	135	11	10	0	6	1.6	0	.25	.09	1.5	—
Canned, spiced or unspiced	2 oz.	57	165	8	14	1	5	1.2	0	.18	.12	1.6	—

NUTRITIVE VALUES OF THE EDIBLE PARTS OF FOODS

Food, approximate measure, and weight (in grams)		Food Energy	Protein	Fat	Carbo-hydrate	Cal-cium	Iron	Vita-min A	Thia-min	Ribo-flavin	Nia-cin	Ascorbic Acid
	Grams	Calories	Grams	Grams	Grams	Milli-grams	Milli-grams	Inter-national units	Milli-grams	Milli-grams	Milli-grams	Milli-grams
Meat, Poultry, Fish, Shellfish; Related Products (continued)												
Sausage:												
Bologna, slice, 3-in. diam. by 1/8 in. .... 2 slices	26	80	3	7	Trace	2	.5	—	.04	.06	.7	—
Frankfurter, heated (8 per lb. purchased pkg.).. 1 frank	56	170	7	15	1	3	.8	—	.08	.11	1.4	—
Pork links, cooked (16 links per lb. raw) ..... 2 links	26	125	5	11	Trace	2	.6	0	.21	.09	1.0	—
Salami, cooked .... 1 oz.	28	90	5	7	Trace	3	.7	—	.07	.07	1.2	—
Fish and shellfish:												
Haddock, breaded, fried .... 3 oz.	85	140	17	5	5	34	1.0	—	.03	.06	2.7	2
Ocean perch, breaded, fried .... 3 oz.	85	195	16	11	6	28	1.1	—	.08	.09	1.5	—
Tuna, canned in oil, drained solids ...... 3 oz.	85	170	24	7	0	7	1.6	70	.04	.10	10.1	—
Mature Dry Beans and Peas, Nuts, Peanuts; Related Products												
Almonds, shelled .... 1 cup	142	850	26	77	28	332	6.7	0	.34	1.31	5.0	Trace
Beans:												
Canned, solids and liquid:												
White with pork and tomato sauce ... 1 cup	255	310	16	7	49	138	4.6	330	.20	.08	1.5	5
Red kidney .... 1 cup	255	230	15	1	42	74	4.6	10	.13	.10	1.5	—
Cashew nuts, roasted .... 1 cup	140	785	24	64	41	53	5.3	140	.60	.35	2.5	—
Peanuts, roasted, salted, halves ..... 1 cup	144	840	37	72	27	107	3.0	—	.46	.19	24.7	0
Peanut butter .... 1 tbsp.	16	95	4	8	3	9	.3	—	.02	.02	2.4	0

Food	Measure											
Pecans, halves	1 cup	108	740	10	77	16	79	2.6	140	.93	.14	1.0	2
Walnuts, chopped	1 cup	126	790	26	75	19	Trace	7.6	380	.28	.14	.9	—

Vegetables and Vegetable Products

Food	Measure											
Beans:												
Green:												
Canned, solids and liquid	1 cup	239	45	2	Trace	10	81	2.9	690	.07	.10	.7	10
Snap, yellow or wax:												
Canned, solids and liquid	1 cup	239	45	2	1	10	81	2.9	140	.07	.10	.7	12
Beets, canned, solids and liquid	1 cup	246	85	2	Trace	19	34	1.5	20	.02	.05	.2	7
Broccoli, cooked, drained:												
Chopped, yield from 10-oz. frozen pkg.	1 3/8 cups	250	65	7	1	12	135	1.8	6,500	.15	.30	1.3	143
Cabbage, raw:												
Finely shredded or chopped	1 cup	90	20	1	Trace	5	44	.4	120	.05	.05	.3	42
Carrots, raw:												
Whole, 5½ by 1 in.	1 carrot	50	20	1	Trace	5	18	.4	5,500	.03	.03	.3	4
Celery, raw:												
Stalk, large outer, 8 by about 1½ in. at root end.	1 stalk	40	5	Trace	Trace	2	16	.1	100	.01	.01	.1	4
Corn, sweet:												
Canned, solids and liquid	1 cup	256	170	5	2	40	10	1.0	690	.07	.12	2.3	13
Cucumbers, 10-oz. 7½ by about 2 in.:												
Raw, pared	1 cucumber	207	30	1	Trace	7	35	.6	Trace	.07	.09	.4	23
Lettuce, raw:												
Boston	1 head	220	30	3	Trace	6	77	4.4	2,130	.14	.13	.6	18
Iceberg, 4 3/4-in. diameter	1 head	454	60	4	Trace	13	91	2.3	1,500	.29	.27	1.3	29
Peas, green; cooked:	1 cup	160	115	9	1	19	37	2.9	860	.44	.17	3.7	33
Peppers, green, raw, about 5 per lb.	1 pod	74	15	1	Trace	4	7	.5	310	.06	.06	.4	94

NUTRITIVE VALUES OF THE EDIBLE PARTS OF FOODS

Food, approximate measure, and weight (in grams)		Food Energy	Protein	Fat	Carbohydrate	Calcium	Iron	Vitamin A	Thiamin	Riboflavin	Niacin	Ascorbic Acid
	Grams	Calories	Grams	Grams	Grams	Milligrams	Milligrams	International units	Milligrams	Milligrams	Milligrams	Milligrams
Vegetables and Vegetable Products (continued)												
Potatoes, medium (about 3 per pound raw):												
Boiled:												
Peeled after boiling · · · · · · · · · · 1 potato	136	105	3	Trace	23	10	.8	Trace	.13	.05	2.0	22
Mashed:												
Milk and butter added · · · · · 1 cup	195	185	4	8	24	47	.8	330	.16	.10	1.9	18
Potato chips, medium, 2-in. diameter · · · 10 chips	20	115	1	8	10	8	.4	Trace	.04	.01	1.0	3
Radishes, raw, small · · · · · · · · 4 radishes	40	5	Trace	Trace	1	12	.4	Trace	.01	.01	.1	10
Tomatoes, raw, approx. 3-in. diameter · · 1 tomato	200	40	2	Trace	9	24	.9	1,640	.11	.07	1.3	42
Tomato juice, canned · · · · · · 1 glass (6 fl. oz.)	182	35	2	Trace	8	13	1.6	1,460	.09	.05	1.5	29
Fruits and Fruit Products												
Apples, raw (about 3 per lb.) · · · · · 1 apple	150	70	Trace	Trace	18	8	.4	50	.04	.02	.1	3
Apple juice, bottled or canned · · · 1 cup	248	120	Trace	Trace	30	15	1.5	—	.02	.05	.2	2
Applesauce, canned, sweetened · · · · 1 cup	255	230	1	Trace	61	10	1.3	100	.05	.03	.1	3
Apricots:												
Raw (about 12 per lb.) · · · · · · 3 apricots	114	55	1	Trace	14	18	.5	2,890	.03	.04	.7	10
Canned in heavy syrup · · · · · 1 cup	259	220	2	Trace	57	28	.8	4,510	.05	.06	.9	10
Apricot nectar, canned · · · · · · 1 cup	251	140	1	Trace	37	23	.5	2,380	.03	.03	.5	8
Bananas raw medium · · · · · · 1 banana	175	100	1	Trace	26	10	9	230	06	07	9	12

Food, approximate measure	Grams	Food energy (Calories)	Protein (g)	Fat (g)	Carbohydrate (g)	Calcium (mg)	Iron (mg)	Vitamin A (I.U.)	Thiamine (mg)	Riboflavin (mg)	Niacin (mg)	Ascorbic acid (mg)
... about 1 2/3 lbs. ... ½ melon	385	60	1	Trace	14	27	.8	6,540	.08	.06	1.2	63
Cranberry juice cocktail, canned ... 1 cup	250	165	Trace	Trace	42	13	.8	Trace	.03	.03	.1	40
Dates, pitted, cut ... 1 cup	178	490	4	1	130	105	5.3	90	.16	.17	3.9	0
Grapefruit: Raw, medium, 3 3/4-in. diameter, white ... 1 grapefruit	241	45	1	Trace	12	19	.5	10	.05	.02	0.2	44
Canned, syrup pack ... 1 cup	254	180	2	Trace	45	33	.8	30	.08	.05	.5	76
Grapefruit juice: Fresh ... 1 cup	246	95	1	Trace	23	22	.5	(11)	.09	.04	.4	92
Canned, white: Unsweetened ... 1 cup	247	100	1	Trace	24	20	1.0	20	.07	.04	.4	84
Sweetened ... 1 cup	250	130	1	Trace	32	20	1.0	20	.07	.04	.4	78
Frozen, concentrate, unsweetened, diluted with 3 parts water by volume ... 1 cup	247	100	1	Trace	24	25	.2	20	.10	.04	.5	96
Lemon juice, raw ... 1 cup	244	60	1	Trace	20	17	.5	50	.07	.02	.2	112
Lemonade concentrate: Frozen, 6 fl. oz. per can ... 1 can	219	430	Trace	Trace	112	9	.4	40	.04	.07	.7	66
Diluted with 4 1/3 parts water, by volume ... 1 cup	248	110	Trace	Trace	28	2	Trace	Trace	Trace	.02	.2	17
Lime juice: Fresh ... 1 cup	246	65	1	Trace	22	22	.5	20	.05	.02	.2	79
Canned, unsweetened ... 1 cup	246	65	1	Trace	22	22	.5	20	.05	.02	.2	52
Limeade concentrate, frozen: Diluted with 4 1/3 parts water, by volume ... 1 cup	247	100	Trace	Trace	27	2	Trace	Trace	Trace	Trace	Trace	5
Oranges, raw, 2 5/8-in. diameter ... 1 orange	180	65	1	Trace	16	54	.5	260	.13	.05	.5	66
Orange juice: Fresh, all varieties ... 1 cup	248	110	2	1	26	27	.5	500	.22	.07	1.0	124
Frozen concentrate, diluted with 3 parts water by volume ... 1 cup	249	120	2	Trace	29	25	.2	550	.22	.02	1.0	120

NUTRITIVE VALUES OF THE EDIBLE PARTS OF FOODS

Food, approximate measure, and weight (in grams)		Food Energy	Protein	Fat	Carbo-hydrate	Cal-cium	Iron	Vita-min A	Thia-min	Ribo-flavin	Nia-cin	Ascorbic Acid
	Grams	Calories	Grams	Grams	Grams	Milli-grams	Milli-grams	Inter-national units	Milli-grams	Milli-grams	Milli-grams	Milli-grams
Fruits and Fruit Products (continued)												
Orange-apricot juice drink . . . . . . 1 cup	249	125	1	Trace	32	12	.2	1,440	.05	.02	.5	40
Orange and grapefruit juice:												
Frozen concentrate diluted with 3 part water by volume . . . . 1 cup	248	110	1	Trace	26	20	.2	270	.16	.02	.8	102
Peaches:												
Raw, whole, medium, 2-in. diameter . . . . 1 peach	114	35	1	Trace	10	9	.5	1,320	.02	.05	1.0	7
Canned, yellow-fleshed, solids and liquid:												
Syrup pack, heavy, halves or slices . . . . 1 cup	257	200	1	Trace	52	10	.8	1,100	.02	.06	1.4	7
Pears:												
Raw, 3 by 2½-in. diameter . . . . 1 pear	182	100	1	1	25	13	.5	30	.04	.07	.2	7
Canned, solids and liquid:												
Syrup pack, heavy, halves or slices . . . . 1 cup	255	195	1	1	50	13	.5	Trace	.03	.05	.3	4
Pineapple:												
Canned, syrup pack, heavy, solids and liquid:												
Crushed . . . . 1 cup	260	195	1	Trace	50	29	.8	120	.20	.06	.5	17
Sliced . . . . 1 large slice	122	90	Trace	Trace	24	13	.4	50	.09	.03	.2	8
Pineapple juice, canned . . . . 1 cup	249	135	1	Trace	34	37	.7	120	.12	.04	.5	22
Plums, all except prunes:												
Raw, 2 in. diameter . . . . 1 plum	60	25	Trace	Trace	7	7	.3	140	.02	.02	.3	3
Canned, syrup pack, with pits and juice . . . . 1 cup	256	205	1	Trace	53	22	2.2	2,970	.05	.05	.9	4

Food	Weight (g)	Calories	(4)	(Trace)	(128)	(102)	(5.8)	(30)	.18	.13	.8	2
Raisins, cup, pressed down . . . . 1 cup	165	480	4	Trace	128	102	5.8	30	.18	.13	.8	2
Strawberries:												
Raw, capped . . . . 1 cup	149	55	1	1	13	31	1.5	90	.04	.10	1.0	88
Frozen, 10-oz. carton, not thawed . . . . . . 1 carton	284	310	1	1	79	40	2.0	90	.06	.17	1.5	150
Tangerines, raw, medium . . . . 1 tangerine	116	40	1	Trace	10	34	.3	360	.05	.02	.1	27
Watermelon, raw, 4 by 8 in. . . . . 1 wedge	925	115	2	1	27	30	2.1	2,510	.13	.13	.7	30

Grain Products

Food												
Bran flakes with raisins, added thiamin and iron . . 1 cup	50	145	4	1	40	28	13.5	Trace	.16	.07	2.7	0
Breads:												
Boston brown bread, slice 3 by 3/4 in. . . . . . . 1 slice	48	100	3	1	22	43	.9	0	.05	.03	.6	0
Cracked wheat bread, 18 slices per loaf . . . . 1 slice	25	65	2	1	13	22	.3	Trace	.03	.02	.3	Trace
French or Vienna bread, enriched, 1-lb. loaf . . . 1 loaf	454	1,315	41	14	251	195	10.0	Trace	1.27	1.00	11.3	Trace
Italian bread, enriched, 1-lb. loaf . . . . 1 loaf	454	1,250	41	4	256	77	10.0	0	1.32	.91	11.8	0
Raisin bread, slice, 18 slices per loaf . . . . . 1 slice	25	65	2	1	13	18	.3	Trace	.01	.02	.2	Trace
Rye bread, American, light, slice, 18 slices per loaf . . . . 1 slice	25	60	2	Trace	13	19	.4	0	.05	.02	.4	0
Pumpernickel, loaf, 1 lb. . . . . 1 loaf	454	1,115	41	5	241	381	10.9	0	1.04	.64	5.4	0
White bread, enriched:												
Soft-crumb type, slice, 18 slices per loaf . . . 1 slice	25	70	2	1	13	21	.6	Trace	.06	.05	.6	Trace
Firm-crumb type, slice, 20 slices per loaf . . . 1 slice	23	65	2	1	12	22	.6	Trace	.06	.05	.6	Trace
Whole wheat bread:												
Soft-crumb type, slice, 16 slices per loaf . . . 1 slice	28	65	3	1	14	24	.8	Trace	.09	.03	.8	Trace
Firm-crumb type, slice, 18 slices per loaf . . . 1 slice	25	60	3	1	12	25	.8	Trace	.06	.03	.7	Trace
Cakes made from cake mixes:												
Cupcakes, small, 2½ in. diameter, without icing . 1 cupcake	25	90	1	3	14	40	.1	40	.01	.03	.1	Trace

NUTRITIVE VALUES OF THE EDIBLE PARTS OF FOODS

Food, approximate measure, and weight (in grams)		Food Energy	Protein	Fat	Carbo-hydrate	Cal-cium	Iron	Vita-min A	Thia-min	Ribo-flavin	Nia-cin	Ascorbic Acid
	Grams	Calories	Grams	Grams	Grams	Milli-grams	Milli-grams	Inter-national units	Milli-grams	Milli-grams	Milli-grams	Milli-grams
Grain Products (continued)												
Cookies:												
Brownies with nuts made from mix . . . . . 1 brownie	20	85	1	4	13	9	.4	20	.03	.02	.1	Trace
Chocolate chip:												
Made from recipe with enriched flour . . . . . 1 cookie	10	50	1	3	6	4	.2	10	.01	.01	.1	Trace
Commercial . . . . 1 cookie	10	50	1	2	7	4	.2	10	Trace	Trace	Trace	Trace
Fig bars, commercial . . . . 1 cookie	14	50	1	1	11	11	.2	20	Trace	.01	.1	Trace
Sandwich, chocolate or vanilla, commercial . . . 1 cookie	10	50	1	2	7	2	.1	0	Trace	Trace	.1	0
Corn (hominy) grits, degermed, cooked, enriched . . . . . . 1 cup	245	125	3	Trace	27	2	.7	150	.10	.07	1.0	0
Corn meal, degermed, enriched:												
Dry form . . . . . . 1 cup	138	500	11	2	108	8	4.0	610	.61	.36	4.8	0
Cooked . . . . . . 1 cup	240	120	3	1	26	2	1.0	140	.14	.10	1.2	0
Corn muffins . . . . . 1 muffin	40	130	3	4	20	96	.6	100	.07	.08	.6	Trace
Crackers:												
Graham, 2½-in. square . . . . . 4 crackers	28	110	2	3	21	11	.4	0	.01	.06	.4	0
Saltines . . . . 4 crackers	11	50	1	1	8	2	.1	0	Trace	Trace	.1	0
Farina, quick-cooking, enriched, cooked . . . . . . 1 cup	245	105	3	Trace	22	147	.7	0	.12	.07	1.0	0
Muffins, with enriched white flour . . . . . 1 muffin	40	120	3	4	17	42	.6	40	.07	.09	.6	Trace
Oatmeal or rolled oats, cooked . . . . . 1 cup	240	130	5	2	23	22	1.4	0	.19	.05	.2	0

Food	Measure	Weight (g)	Calories	Protein	Fat	Carbohydrate	Calcium	Iron	Vitamin A	Thiamin	Riboflavin	Niacin	Ascorbic acid
Rice, white, instant, ready to serve	1 cup	165	180	4	Trace	40	5	1.3	0	.21	—	1.7	0
Rolls, enriched:													
Frankfurter or hamburger	1 roll	40	120	3	2	21	30	.8	Trace	.11	.07	.9	Trace
Hard, round or rectangular	1 roll	50	155	5	2	30	24	1.2	Trace	.13	.12	1.4	Trace
Waffles, made from mix, enriched, egg and milk added, 7-in. diameter	1 waffle	75	205	7	8	27	179	1.0	170	.11	.17	.7	Trace
Wheat, puffed, added nutrients	1 cup	15	55	2	Trace	12	4	.6	0	.08	.03	1.2	0
Wheat, shredded, plain	1 biscuit	25	90	2	1	20	11	.9	0	.06	.03	1.1	0
Wheat flakes, added nutrients	1 cup	30	105	3	Trace	24	12	1.3	0	.19	.04	1.5	0

Fats, Oils

Food	Measure	Weight (g)	Calories	Protein	Fat	Carbohydrate	Calcium	Iron	Vitamin A	Thiamin	Riboflavin	Niacin	Ascorbic acid
Butter:													
Regular, 4 sticks per pound													
Stick	½ cup	113	810	1	92	1	23	0	3,750	—	—	—	0
Tablespoon (approx. 1/8 stick)	1 tbsp.	14	100	Trace	12	Trace	3	0	470	—	—	—	0
Margarine:													
Regular, 4 sticks per pound													
Stick	½ cup	113	815	1	92	1	23	0	3,750	—	—	—	0
Tablespoon (approx. 1/8 stick)	1 tbsp.	14	100	Trace	12	Trace	3	0	470	—	—	—	0
Salad dressing:													
Commercial, mayonnaise type	1 tbsp.	15	65	Trace	6	2	2	Trace	30	Trace	Trace	Trace	—
French	1 tbsp.	16	65	Trace	6	3	2	.1	—	—	—	—	—
Mayonnaise	1 tbsp.	14	100	Trace	11	Trace	3	.1	40	Trace	.01	Trace	—

Sugars, Sweets

Food	Measure	Weight (g)	Calories	Protein	Fat	Carbohydrate	Calcium	Iron	Vitamin A	Thiamin	Riboflavin	Niacin	Ascorbic acid
Chocolate-flavored syrup or topping:													
Thin type	1 fl. oz.	38	90	1	1	24	6	.6	Trace	.01	.03	.2	0
Fudge type	1 fl. oz.	38	125	2	5	20	48	.5	60	.02	.08	.2	Trace

NUTRITIVE VALUES OF THE EDIBLE PARTS OF FOODS

Food, approximate measure, and weight (in grams)		Food Energy	Protein	Fat	Carbo-hydrate	Cal-cium	Iron	Vita-min A	Thia-min	Ribo-flavin	Nia-cin	Ascorbic Acid
	Grams	Calories	Grams	Grams	Grams	Milli-grams	Milli-grams	Inter-national units	Milli-grams	Milli-grams	Milli-grams	Milli-grams
Sugars, Sweets (continued)												
Chocolate-flavored beverage powder (approx. 4 heaping tsp. per oz.):												
with non-fat dry milk · · · · · · · 1 oz.	28	100	5	1	20	167	.5	10	.04	.21	.2	1
Honey, strained or extracted · · · · 1 tbsp.	21	65	Trace	0	17	1	.1	0	Trace	.01	.1	Trace
Jams and preserves · · · · · · · · · 1 tbsp.	20	55	Trace	Trace	14	4	.2	Trace	Trace	.01	Trace	Trace
Jellies · · · · · · · · · · · · · 1 tbsp.	18	50	Trace	Trace	13	4	.3	Trace	Trace	.01	Trace	1
Molasses, cane:												
Light (first extraction) · · · · · · 1 tbsp.	20	50	—	—	13	33	.9	—	.01	.01	Trace	—
Blackstrap (third extraction) · · 1 tbsp.	20	45	—	—	11	137	3.2	—	.02	.04	.4	—
Sugars:												
Brown, firm packed · · · · · · · · 1 cup	220	820	0	0	212	187	7.5	0	.02	.07	.4	0
White, granulated · · · · · · · · · 1 cup	200	770	0	0	199	0	.2	0	0	0	0	0
· · · · · · · · · · · · · 1 tbsp.	11	40	0	0	11	0	Trace	0	0	0	0	0
Syrups, table blends, chiefly corn, light and dark · · 1 tbsp.	21	60	0	0	15	9	.8	0	0	0	0	0
Miscellaneous Items												
Barbecue sauce · · · · · · · · · · 1 cup	250	230	4	17	20	53	2.0	900	.03	.03	.8	13
*Instant puddings: Banana, butterscotch, French vanilla,	169	178	4.2	4.7	20.5	144		182	.04	.21	0.1	1

Coconut cream . . . . ½ cup	149	188	4.5	6.1	29.0	145	.1	183	.04	.21	0.1	1

Soups:

Prepared with an equal volume of water: Bean with pork . . . . 1 cup	250	170	8	6	22	63	2.3	650	.13	.08	1.0	3
Dehydrated, dry form: Chicken noodle (2-oz. pkg.) . . . . 1 pkg.	57	220	8	6	33	34	1.4	190	.30	.15	2.4	3

* Your Chart of Food Values
General Food Kitchens

index